The Zen of Strategy

Applying game theory and Buddhist principles to maximise ethical success at both work and at home

by

Kenji Maeda
© Copyright Kenji Maeda 2013
All Rights Reserved

Table of Contents

Introduction 3
Chapter One – Attachment 7
Chapter Two - Mindfulness 14
Chapter Three – The Law of Karma 21
Chapter Four - Impermanence 28
Chapter Five – The Middle Way 32
Chapter Six – Non-Harm 35
Conclusion 38
Recommended Reading 39

Introduction

At first glance, the idea of linking Buddhism with game theory may seem incongruous. Buddhism is typically associated with altruism and selfless action, while game theory is concerned with the maximisation of personal gain via strategic thought and action. However, if you dig a little deeper, the parallels become more obvious. Both fields have a strong emphasis on logic and the value of empirical verification, bringing a solid framework to models of behaviour and decision making. It soon becomes clear that these two *philosophies* (if you can call them that), are not mutually exclusive and proponents of each can benefit from applying concepts from the other.

You may notice that this book (or whatever the non-fiction version of a novella is!) is brief and to the point, with an accordingly frugal page count. There are two reasons for this. Firstly, as an avid consumer of both Buddhist and game theory related literature I consistently find myself skimming through unnecessary background and detail to reach the key message. I often get the impression that content that does not add anything meaningful is added to beef up word counts in many books. Therefore, my editing has been brutal, chopping out anything which does not add anything of note to the overall message of the book. Secondly, I believe that my severe editing is in keeping with the spirit of Zen which says *if something isn't important, drop it*. Zen philosophy preaches the beauty of brevity and simplicity, which I believe this document upholds.

There are already innumerable books on the subjects of Buddhism and game theory, written by those significantly more adept than I at practicing and preaching each. I have therefore not gone into too much detail describing the history and theory of these topics, but have included a *Recommended Reading* section at the back of the book for those who wish to deepen their understanding.

Before we move on, let me mention the title. As most people would know, *Zen* is only one branch of Buddhism and the majority of the concepts in this book are general Buddhist concepts rather than specifically Zen. However I have called this book *The Zen of Strategy* for two reasons. Firstly, Zen is the most empirical and purely psychological in focus of all the different branches of Buddhism. It avoids too much focus on the metaphysical aspects of Buddhism such as reincarnation and the various "hell" and "heaven" realms. This makes it a good fit for the avid game theorist. I don't want to scare off a prospective game theorist by detailing the purpose of *Kasinas* or the purgatory realm of *Bardo*! Secondly, I have to practice what I preach, and by mapping out the chain of cause and effect of various titles, such as *Dharma Strategy* or *Buddhist Strategy*, I found that *The Zen of Strategy* is the clearest and has the best chance of finding an audience. Pragmatism must always win.

So, what is "game theory"?

Put simply, game theory is the study of strategic decision-making. It often uses mathematical models to represent the differing ways that the decisions of each party are interrelated in a strategic interaction.

So first things first - we need to define a strategic interaction. Negotiation is the typical example of a strategic interaction; however in reality a great deal of all your interactions will require strategic thinking.

What is *strategic thinking*? Prominent game theorists Avinash Dixit and Barry Nalebuff call strategic thinking *"...the art of outdoing an adversary, knowing that the adversary is trying to do the same to you..."* This can be a commercial negotiation such as selling your house, a decision on the best route to take to work or even a nuclear arms race. Any situation where two or more parties need to make decisions to maximise a particular outcome. Put another way, you make your decision based on what you expect from the other "player" in the game.

The classic (and dare I say it, overused) example of a strategic interaction is called *The Prisoner's Dilemma*. In this theoretical game, two men are arrested as suspects for a particular crime, however the police do not have sufficient evidence to convict either of them. The men are separated and then both offered a deal – if one of them testifies and the other remains silent, the man who co-operates will walk free and the other will receive a 10 year prison term. If both remain silent, they each receive a 1 year term. If both confess, they each receive a 3 year term. Neither man knows what the other has said or will say. From an overall perspective, the correct decision is for each to remain silent as the total time spent in jail is 2 years (1 year for each person). However, the most logical decision for each man to make individually is to confess and rat out the other, risking a maximum of 3 years. Note that any decision apart from "both stay silent", leads to more aggregate jail time when you combine both men.

The Prisoner's Dilemma is a highly simplified interaction. It does not address key factors such as – each person's level of credibility based on past actions (is either of the men known as being strong and stoic or easily broken?) or any particular arrangement put in place prior to arrest which would have ensured that both stay silent (such as an arrangement with a third-party to harm family members in the event of a confession by either man). However it does give a flavour of how the likely decisions of others need to be considered when making your own decision in a particular scenario.

The Buddhist "Angle"

Buddhism requires less explanation. While commonly referred to as a religion, it rarely conforms to any of the criteria for defining a religion. In particular, it has little in common with the world's primary monotheistic faiths such as Christianity and Islam. There is no single omnipotent God and no eternal, unchanging soul. Buddhism emphasises the attainment of enlightenment through personal effort and introspection via various forms of meditation. What Buddhism does have in common with traditional religions is that it has a strong focus on the importance of ethical and moral behaviour.

So where does Buddhism intersect with game theory?

Well, I believe that by combining the application of certain Buddhist practices alongside existing game theory based strategies, you can maximise your chances of success in various arenas of your business and personal life. Furthermore, whilst the bulk of this book focuses on business and commercial matters, these concepts can also be applied to other aspects of your life.

Now, let me address the question which may have arisen in your mind – *Is it not perverse to apply Buddhist concepts to the area of maximising commercial gain? After all, under the Buddhist concept of anatta (no self), isn't it just the universe competing with the universe?*

Firstly, most interactions are not *zero-sum* games (games which are binary – there is a winner and a loser). Most interactions in life are to some extent *co-operative*. This means that the skilful application of Buddhist and game theory principles can result in a better net result for all participants. This allows the use of the over-abused business expression *win-win*. Applying the principles in this book creates the game-plan for all participants to extract a better result from a given scenario.

For example, say there are two people living in the wilderness who need to eat. They have the option of each of them working alone to catch rabbits and other small prey (1 unit of food each) or co-operating to take down a buffalo together (10 units of food combined). Just like *The Prisoner's Dilemma*, co-operation generates much better return than working independently or against each other. Secondly, we need to be pragmatic in terms of an individual's motivations. Whilst the end goal of Buddhist practice is to reach a state of pure selflessness in terms of motivation, a worthy intermediate goal can be the same behaviours, but with the goal of maximising personal gain. For example, say you decide to give $20 to a homeless person on the street. Whether you would care to admit it or not, for the majority of people, bundled up with this action is the knowledge that you will feel better as a person and pleasure is derived from the reaction of this homeless person to receiving a windfall from you. Or put another way, you could be paying the $20 to avoid the unpleasant feeling that would potentially arise after witnessing the reaction of the homeless person to your perceived lack of generosity.

One level up from this in terms of "pureness" is where you do something with no expectation of personal recognition. A couple of real world examples of this is where some people walk around the city putting coins into expired meters or people that pay the road toll of the car behind them.

In Buddhist practice, the eventual goal is to give from a place of complete selflessness - to have no expectation of psychological or material gain from the act of giving. However, if one was to remain dogmatic and pursue this as a singular goal, it would be a shame, as it is an exceedingly difficult endeavour. At the end of the day, if you follow a Buddhist philosophy in life, it will result in a net benefit to the world, irrespective of your underlying motivations. This is why I believe there should be no shame in applying Buddhist principles to commercial life.

Chapter One – Attachment

The Four Noble Truths

Perhaps the central teaching of Buddhism is known as The Four Noble Truths. Put simply, the general gist of it is -

1. Life is suffering
2. The cause of suffering is craving and attachment
3. It is possible to eliminate suffering
4. The way to eliminate suffering is by following *The Eightfold Path*. Put another way – if you follow the key guidelines of Buddhism, craving can be overcome.

A lot of people get to the first part of the Four Noble Truths and think *"wow this Buddhism stuff is depressing – first they tell me I have no soul and there is no heaven and now they lay this on me – I'm outta here!"* However this is a shame because what it is saying is really quite simple and intuitive. Ram Dass put it best when he said *"if you don't crave something, you can't suffer about it"*.

Let me use the example of an ice-cream. Say you decide to head down to the ice-cream shop to buy your favourite ice-cream, *The Quad-Choctastic Fantasy Mouth Explosion*, however the only flavour they have left remaining *is The Vanilla Bourbon Bean Oral Assault*. If you crave the chocolate (relative to the vanilla) you are then going to suffer. If, however, you are completely ambivalent as to which flavour you have, you will not suffer.

So then you think, *"Wow! I have mastered the Four Noble Truths – now to move on to astral travel"*. However, what happens then if you find out they don't have either flavour? That's right, no ice-cream at all. There's suffering again. Unless of course you don't care either way between eating ice-cream and say, a bar of chocolate. But what happens if....as you can see, it keeps going.

Here's where it gets truly diabolical.

Say, they did have your favourite flavour and you have just finished the cone. Yep, suffering again. Your ice-cream is now gone. Put another way, any pleasurable experience is impermanent and based in time. A great example of this is when you get into a Japanese hot spring on a cold winter's day or lay down in bed after a day of high-activity or hard labour. What is initially intensely pleasurable eventually can become torture. Eventually the water becomes intolerably hot or your position in bed becomes uncomfortable. Next time you lay down in bed, try to see what happens if you do not move at all for a long period. Pleasure will eventually turn to discomfort, despite you not doing anything. However if you move into a new position, pleasure starts once again and the time clock starts ticking again. Another example is that moment during a relaxing vacation when you realise that the vacation will end soon and you will have to return to work. You got what you want but it is always impermanent so consequently there is suffering even embedded in pleasure. Long story short – it is impossible to hold on to pleasurable feelings and experiences so the key is not to crave them or be attached to them.

It is beyond the scope of this book to go into the process of how to completely eliminate craving (assuming you even wanted to) as per Buddhist teachings. However, the general concept is that with enough focused and concentrated contemplation on the nature of reality, eventually you realise the *empty* nature of phenomena. Life is just a play of light, sound and touch with no inherent substance. A good way to explain this is to imagine that life is just a movie which you are watching and experiencing through your various senses. Think about the level of emotional reaction you have to something in a movie such as some kind of tragedy befalling star-crossed lovers or the death of a character in a film. Now compare this to the level of emotional reaction (or *attachment*) if this happens to you in real life. So what would happen if you were to slowly view your own life as a kind of movie which you were viewing as a third-person? It is hard to maintain for long periods of time, however I recommend trying it. Go into a meeting at work and try to maintain a third-person perspective, viewing the events of the meeting as a movie or play. Do it enough times and you find that a lot of the emotional sting comes out of various events.

Optionality

If someone was to ask me what is the most important thing to consider when heading into a strategic interaction (particularly a commercial negotiation), I would say -

1. Don't be in a position where you have no options or alternatives

2. Don't put yourself in a situation where you are under time pressure to act or decide

Let me use the example of buying a car. Based on above, how are you best served when embarking on an imminent vehicle purchase?

Firstly, have options. Widen your search sufficiently – both geographically (include a wide area with plenty of car dealers) and by specification (don't be too specific in what kind of car you want – either by colour, make or model). If you have your heart set on a particular car at a particular dealer, you are setting yourself up to come off second best in your negotiation with the car dealer. Taken to the extreme, if you are then insane enough to signal to the car dealer that your heart is set on this particular car, you probably shouldn't be driving a motor vehicle or handling sharp objects.

Secondly, have time. To continue with the car buying analogy, you need to allow yourself the luxury of time. At one extreme, you decide to leisurely look for a bargain over a long period of time and at the other extreme, you decide (or don't prepare and are forced) to buy a car that very day, no matter what. I don't think I need to tell you which of these scenarios will lead you to overpaying.

In commercial trade, the classical application of this concept is in commodity trading. In this example, let's say you are now the seller and you have 60,000 tonnes of Commodity X you own and want to sell. Your competitor, Mr Y, contacts you to see if you have any Commodity X to sell.

So, to optimise your position, you first need to make sure you have 'options'. The obvious route to achieve this is to make sure you are talking to multiple buyers simultaneously. You can then either coax a one time, auction style bid out of each party or engage in several rounds of negotiation to get the best price for your Commodity X.

Next, you need to make sure you have time on your side. Again, the best way to illustrate this is to talk in terms of extremes. Say, for example that due to its risk management protocols, your company only allows you to hold a maximum of 50,000 tonnes of Commodity X at 'close of business' (COB) each day. This robs you of the 'time' dimension, as you will need to sell at least 10,000 tonnes that day, no matter what. If you are still 'long' 60,000 tonnes of Commodity X at 4.30pm, you will be forced to take whatever price you are offered, without the luxury of getting the best possible price. God forbid that your competitor knows your true situation. In that case you are going to have to bite down on some kind of chew strap and put on some soothing music because it is certainly not going to be gentle. It is in fact this very scenario which was seen during the Global Financial Crisis (GFC) when financial institutions were forced to unwind extensive derivative positions in a hurry. You really want to avoid this.

Naturally, interactions like this are usually more complex and nuanced. For example, you need to consider what you know about the buyer in the above example. Say you know their stock position is currently 25000 tonnes of Commodity X and you know that the most economical way to transport Commodity X is in 55000 tonne full-sized vessels. Say again for argument's sake that you find out via a shipping company that the buyer has booked a vessel to arrive at the export terminal in 4 weeks. This completely changes the flavour of your interaction with them. Real world scenarios are usually complex in this way.

So by now I guess you know where I am heading with this – in an commercial interaction, one of the keys to success is to ensure you do not become emotionally attached to a particular outcome or course of action. By narrowing the spectrum of different options you will accept or be satisfied with, you are dramatically reducing the probability of success.

Effective strategic interaction requires a reliance on your pre-frontal cortex (the rational thought and planning centre of the brain) rather than your limbic system (emotional centre). Interestingly, this is the brain state promoted by consistent meditation practice. I will talk about this in more detail later however the key point remains that you need to not allow emotional attachment sabotage a carefully planned strategic interaction.

Let me use a recent, real world example which perfectly illustrates the point. Recently we decided to sell our house and move to a smaller house temporarily. There were several reasons but primarily it was to set ourselves up financially to buy a block of land and build our dream house (it would be too expensive to have two big loans at the same time while the next house was being constructed). So, in the interests of practising what I preach, for this transaction (selling our existing house and buying a new, temporary place), we set the following rules -

1. We would follow a strict sequence – list existing house for sale, look for house to buy, sell existing house, buy new house. We would not break the cardinal rule of buying a new house before you have sold your current house. When people do this they lose the time advantage as you risk being forced to take any price at a certain point in time. If we found somewhere perfect (both in terms of price and other criteria) before selling, we could make an offer *subject to sale*.

2. To allow us to keep the time advantage, we put in place two things. We arranged with a relative to rent their empty apartment for a period of time in the event that we sold our house and hadn't found a house to buy. We also instructed the real estate agent to request a 'rent-back' period with any prospective buyer of our house. This would mean that in the above scenario, we could rent back our house until we found a new house. Naturally there are two points to consider regarding above. Firstly, not everyone will have the option to rent a vacant apartment for a month or two. Secondly, by adding a 'rent-back' clause, we were

potentially restricting our pool of buyers. What would happen if one buyer offered $5000 more than the other but would not accept 'rent-back'? Then you need to make some additional decisions and attribute monetary value to your series of options from that point.

3. We would create as wide a 'specification' as possible (the 'options' component) for our new property. Firstly, we created as wide a geographic catchment area as possible with the two factors being the location of our child's school and my office. Then we created a wide specification for the type of property we would target, with as few restrictive criteria as possible

4. Regarding the sale of our existing house and particularly the initial discussions with our real estate agent, I was keen to follow a planned course of action. Firstly, I recognised a basic principle which many people don't seem to realise – despite the fact that you have appointed a real estate agent to represent your interests, they are closer to a 'buyer's' agent rather than a 'seller's' agent for one major reason – real estate agents are not incentivised to get maximum value for the seller; they are incentivised to quickly turn property over. If they extract an extra few thousand dollars for you, their actual share of the upside is inconsequential. It is therefore in their interest to convince you list your property for a low price and then for you to take the first low-ball offer which comes in. (For those interested in reading more on this, I strongly recommend reading Freakonomics by Steven D. Levitt & Stephen J. Dubner)

5. Secondly, I was keen to use the concept of 'anchoring' in early discussions with the agent. Anchoring is a concept identified and popularized by prominent psychologists Daniel Kahneman and Amos Tversky. Anchoring is a type of cognitive bias where your opinion is unduly influenced by a piece of information you have received. For example, in various studies, if people were given a high number as either direct or indirect guidance for a particular answer, they would subsequently guess a higher number than those given low numbers. I was therefore careful to start off discussions with the agent around a number higher than I thought our property was worth. I was also careful to signal very clearly that we were happy to take our time and would only take 'top dollar' for our property. Now, naturally you may say (especially if you are a real estate agent) that this is nothing new – most owners think their property is worth more than it is. In this respect you would be correct, however I also provided no possible avenue for the agent to convince us to take a lower price as I clearly stated that we will only take

top dollar, are happy to be patient and if we do not achieve top dollar we will not sell.

5. Regarding the purchase of the next property, we were careful to make sure that we always had a minimum of two options 'live' at any point, to ensure that we did not overpay due to a lack of options. Naturally, we also carefully signalled to the seller's agent each time that we were considering multiple properties.

So why is this scenario such a good example of being careful not to become emotionally attached to a single option? The family home is naturally a highly emotive topic and it is difficult to divorce emotion from logic when the decision involves your home. At many points during the process, I found myself becoming emotionally attached to a particular option and had to be disciplined to follow the original plan. This is particularly the case when you find a property to buy which is subjectively desirable for various reasons. Now, there is nothing wrong with choosing your home based on subjective criteria if this is where you plan to raise your children or eke out some other form of textbook life long term, however in this case, the property was a means to an end.

A few weeks into this process is where another interesting factor comes into play – *decision fatigue*. This is a phenomenon where decision making is likened to lifting weights – after a period of frequent or high-stakes decision making, the 'decision making muscle' becomes fatigued. If you are not careful, it is at this point where you are at risk of settling for a sub-optimal option as you 'can't be bothered' any more. In our case we were keenly aware of this factor coming into play at several points and had to consciously be mindful to keep it in check.

From my own personal experience, one of the best examples of the dangers of decision fatigue came when I was buying my last car. As anyone who has purchased a new car will attest, just when you thought you were good to go, the car dealer places one last perilous obstacle course in your way – the 'optional extras' pitch. This is where they try to convince you to get all manner of spurious extras such as – custom mud-flaps, sunroof, oil slick to deter would-be pursuers, ejector seats etc.

At this particular car dealer, the optional extras pitch was unusually and brutally comprehensive. It went on for such a long period of time I eventually fell into the *decision fatigue* trap. Right near the end when they know you will be at your weakest point, they unleash "rust proofing". Usually I am primed and ready for the 'rust proofing' pitch and can deal with it accordingly. However in this case they had destroyed my spirit to the point where I would say anything to get out of there and consequently agreed to the rust-proofing. As an aside, it was particularly disappointing because they used another common trick to pitch it to me which I would normally be ready for – instead of quoting the flat price, they told me how much extra it would cost to add to the overall vehicle finance – thereby making a big number seem small by chopping it up and then juxtaposing it against a bigger number (the overall finance). Put another way, an interesting aspect of the 'optional extras' pitch you get when purchasing a vehicle is the way it is cleverly conducted after you have just spent tens of thousands of dollars on a car. I was reminded of this recently when I purchased thousands of dollars' worth of new appliances for my kitchen. One small item was only worth $200 and I just couldn't be bothered haggling to get a better price. Luckily, without even asking, the sales assistance gave us a $50 discount. As I was walking out of the store I remembered a week earlier in the same store, haggling in earnest for $30 off the price of a $300 coffee machine. When you spend thousands, $50 suddenly doesn't seem like much.

So by now, you grasp the concept of attachment and why you need to avoid it, however how do you then go about putting it into practice? That's where the miracle of mindfulness comes in.

Chapter Two - Mindfulness

Mindfulness is the act of being present and attentive to what is happening in the 'now'. It is perhaps best described by giving an example of both mindfulness itself and its opposite state. The varying ways we consume food is a great medium for explaining mindfulness. Go into your kitchen and grab a small amount of your favourite food such as chocolate or strawberries (or whatever else tickles your fancy). Put it in your mouth and savour every aspect of it – the flavours, the mouth-feel – everything. Eat it very slowly.

Jon Kabat-Zinn, pioneer of *Mindfulness Based Stress Reduction* (MBSR), uses the humble raisin for this exercise. When you think about it, how often do you consume food in this way? Unfortunately, the opposite of mindfulness example is more likely to be familiar to you. How often have you consumed something you love (like chocolate etc.), looked down and seen that it is all gone and realised you had been a million miles away and didn't actually taste any of it?

This concept can be applied to anything, not just food. The one which always drives me crazy is when I am looking forward to a nice hot shower, finish the shower and realise that the entire time I was thinking about something else and not enjoying the hedonic aspect of the shower.

The concept of mindfulness (or lack thereof) is a central focus of Buddhist practice. It's staggering to think of the proportion of your life you spend either imagining the future or reliving past events, rather than experiencing the present. Again to use the movie analogy, it is like doing your shopping list while watching a film – you are going to miss all the best parts as your mind is elsewhere.

So why is mindfulness so important in the arena of strategy? Primarily, if you practice mindfulness, you will be able to prevent emotional reactions hijacking your plans.

Firstly, allow me to illustrate by showing you the areas of your brain involved in both planning and the emotional reactions. In the interest of not boring you to tears with too much unnecessary *brain-talk*, I will keep it brief. There is an area of your brain called the pre-frontal cortex (PFC). Think of this as the rational, logical planning area of your brain. Then there is a part of your brain called the limbic system which includes key parts of the 'emotional' brain such as the amygdala and the hippocampus. The hippocampus is usually mentioned as the brain's *memory centre*; however it is a little more complex in reality. One of the key functions of the hippocampus is to detect context. The amygdala is your ancient early-warning system. The amygdala's key function is to give emotional colour (particularly fear) to experience. However, one of the downsides (or upsides, if you are looking at it from an evolutionary perspective) is that the amygdala has a hair trigger. A good example of the amygdala at work is if somebody put a fake spider on your chair. That micro-second where you panic prior to realising that the spider is not real is your amygdala at work. The amygdala is referred to as 'quick and dirty' – meaning – it is not overly accurate – its primary job is to be quick. What then happens is that the sight of the spider has meanwhile taken a longer, circuitous route through the brain until the point, a micro-second later, where you realise that the spider is not real and you can then relax.

In evolutionary terms, your brain has given the limbic system the ability to completely hijack your brain in times where your survival is at stake. If a lion suddenly appears close by, your brain wants you to either 'fight' or 'flee' ('flight'), not to take your time assessing the probabilities of differing courses of action. This is where the term 'fight or flight reaction' comes from.

So where does the hippocampus come in to this discussion? If a particular event is tagged as being important by the amygdala, it is imprinted via extensive connection with the hippocampus. The best example of this is when a soldier returns from war suffering from *Post-Traumatic Stress Disorder* (PTSD). When the soldier hears a car backfire or fireworks go off, it is very similar to the sound of gunfire, which the amygdala and hippocampus have tagged and stored as being something requiring a strong fear reaction. The hippocampus is now also being implicated in a wider range of emotional disorders including depression. One of the hallmarks of depression in the brain is hippocampal atrophy. More interestingly, one of the clearest changes which modern day anti-depressant drugs (such as SSRIs) trigger in the brain is neurogenesis (the birth of new neurons) in the hippocampus. This neuroplastic change in the hippocampus is strongly correlated with the clinical effectiveness of these drugs, strongly pointing to the hippocampus playing a central role in emotional reactivity.

However, as is evidenced by the prevalence of various anxiety disorders such as *Panic Disorder* and *Post Traumatic Stress Disorder* (PTSD), the limbic system is not well suited to modern life. The limbic system is adapted to deal with acute stress (such as being chased by a lion) but not with chronic stress (such as a high pressure business environment). In other ways the limbic system is problematic because, from an evolutionary perspective it has been advantageous for it to over-react to various situations.

One of the prime examples of the limbic system's ability to 'take control of the wheel' is during times of high emotion. The perfect example of this is 'crimes of passion' leading to murder or 'brain-snaps' which are often seen on the sporting field. Anger is particularly adept at hijacking the brain. Evidence of this is seen time and time again in murder trials where a situation of high-emotion inexplicably escalates to murder, with the perpetrator claiming that they 'lost control'. From a neural perspective, this is simply the limbic system temporarily 'taking over the wheel', preventing the PFC from making rational decisions which are in the best interest of the person in question.

Mindfulness practice has been shown to reduce this autonomic reactivity in the brain and allow the PFC to regain control over emotional situations. Both mindfulness practice and *Cognitive Behavioural Therapy* (CBT) make use of the brain's inherent plasticity. Neural Plasticity essentially refers to the brain's ability physically and functionally change in response to experience. A classic example of this is the study by the University College London which involved scanning the brains of London cabbies. These cab drivers exhibited significantly greater activity in the hippocampus which was also reflected in physically larger hippocampi. It was demonstrated via MRI scans that the brains of these drivers had literally grown to accommodate the huge spatial map required to memorise all the streets of London. The results of this study have been replicated in other fields of endeavour also, such as musicians who show greater activity in the parts of the brain controlling hand movement.

Cognitive Behavioural Therapy (CBT) applies the similar principle that repeatedly changing the way you think about certain things and your underlying behaviours, you can slowly extinguish maladaptive habits. The interesting thing about CBT is where it intersects with Buddhist practice in various ways. For example, in the area of anxiety disorders, CBT often focuses on reducing overly emotional reactions to common situations such as flying, public speaking or any other common phobia triggers. Or for people with depressive illnesses, it focuses on reframing certain events, due to the tendency of depressed people to have a negative view of positive or neutral events. It is easy to see the clear overlaps with Buddhist concepts of 'attachment' and 'mindfulness'. As an example, if you were to answer the phone to talk to a telemarketer you would have a completely different physiological and psychological reaction than if you were receiving a call regarding a recent job interview. The difference is your level of attachment to the outcome of each interaction. Put another way, if you are able to reach a state where you are not attached to the outcome of, say, a public speaking engagement, you would naturally not be as anxious.

Buddhist thought says that the central problem is delusion, or a lack of understanding of the underlying nature of things. This is best illustrated by one of my favourite allegories, which I will give a simple version of here -

One day a farmer's only horse runs away.
"How terrible!" said the neighbour
"Good, bad, who knows?" said the farmer
The next day the horse returns with several new horses
"How wonderful!" said the neighbour
"Good, bad, who knows?" said the farmer
The next day, while trying to break in the new horses, the farmer's only son breaks his leg
"How terrible!" said the neighbour
"Good, bad, who knows?" said the farmer
The next day, the army visits the farm to conscript young men for war; however the farmer's son is saved due to his broken leg
"How wonderful!" said the neighbour
"Good, bad, who knows?" said the farmer

At the risk of stating the obvious, the clear message of this story is that it is pointless to get overly emotional about certain events as you have no way of knowing how things will turn out or what else may be at play.

By practising mindfulness, you are able to apply these kinds of logical concepts in various situations, short circuiting your automatic limbic system reactions. However it is crucial to be realistic and keep expectations initially low. It is reasonably easy to maintain control if you are prepared for a potentially emotional event. For example, if you have a meeting scheduled with a particularly disagreeable person, you can practice maintaining mindfulness so that you are ready for any particularly provocative or confronting comments by this person. However many situations are significantly more challenging than this – particularly if you have not had an opportunity to prepare ahead. One of the best examples is to check in for a flight and it has either been cancelled or you have been bumped off the flight. This situation would test even the most seasoned mindfulness exponents.

Gradually, by being mindful you can notice the beginnings of an angry feeling (say, a tightening in your gut or chest). The miracle of mindfulness is that just this simple act of noticing the beginnings of limbic system activity has the effect of reducing its intensity.

In my experience, one of the best ways to cultivate mindfulness is the practice of *Vipassana* meditation. In basic terms, Buddhist meditation practice can be broken up into *Shamatha* (concentration) and *Vipassana* (insight). Shamatha is the aspect of meditation involved in calming down, reducing distraction and growing your powers of concentration. Vipassana is more focused on gaining insight into the workings of the mind and the nature of existence. Neither is more important than the other – they are viewed as legs under a table. Without a certain level of concentration, you will never sufficiently 'penetrate' a subject before becoming distracted and concentration alone is of little use unless it is used to gain genuine insight.

Vipassana alone is a huge topic; however for the purposes of developing your powers of mindfulness, I want to focus on the Vipassana practice of *thought watching*. In this practice, after settling down with some Shamatha meditation (such as counting your in-breath and out-breath), you then just watch your thoughts as they occur. Some key points -

· You don't try to stop your thoughts. This is vital. By trying to stop your thoughts you are implicitly saying that one particular thought is desirable and another is not. Or, put another way, it is saying that having no thoughts at all is good and, by extension, any thinking is bad. You are trying to practice mindfulness and dropping attachment, so you should not allow yourself to become attached to any particular state.

· It is nigh on impossible to stop thoughts so trying to do so is futile. When first trying this, people sometimes think that their thoughts have amplified and have become more frenetic than usual. This is simply a result of turning down the 'signal to noise' ratio – meaning – by slowing down and watching your thoughts, you notice a lot more than you would usually be able to.

· A typical ideal thought process would be just noting thought such as "thinking about what I will have for dinner" or "thinking about an argument I had with a colleague". An often used analogy is of someone hired to count people as they come through the door to a party. You don't care who comes, your job is just to note them down when they come through the door.

- When you note a thought, just return to concentrating on your breathing and watching for more thoughts.

- You WILL get lost in a train of thought quite often so don't get despondent if you keep doing this. Remember, this is just another form of attachment to a particular outcome – for the entire session you need to drop judgement. When you notice you are lost in thought, just notice it and return to your breathing.

- While focusing on the breath, you can either focus on the sensation of the breath entering the nostril or on the belly as it goes in and out.

After a while of regularly practicing mindfulness in these ways, an interesting thing develops. Slowly, a screen comes up between you and your thoughts. For most people, they are their thoughts, indivisible. As Descartes famously (and with debatable veracity) said *I think, therefore I am*. However, slowly a habit develops where a typical thought process may then be *Ah, there I am starting to get angry* or *Ah, there I am thinking negative thoughts*. This quickly takes a lot of the emotional sting out of events as you develop a little third-person perspective on your thoughts.

So eventually, with sustained and focused practice, you will gradually be able to prevent emotions from sabotaging a logical strategic plan. Heading into any important strategic interaction, it would also be helpful to identify potential emotional states that may arise ahead of time, so you are adequately prepared for their occurrence. To use the car purchase example again, you could put yourself of alert for a strong preference starting to emerge for a particular vehicle. Then, using your Mindfulness training, you can identify it as it begins to occur with a thought such as "ah, there I am starting to get too attached to a Toyota Prius".

The beauty of gaining this level of emotional control is that your counter-party in the interaction will be forming their own strategy assuming that you will not have control over emotional reactions. The people selling their house may fill it with luxurious furniture and fill the house with the smell of fresh coffee for the home open, fully expecting it to influence your decision-making process. The perception of the other parties' emotions is central to many strategic interactions. A classic example of this is the concept of *brinkmanship* such as what occurred between the US & Russia during the *Cuban Missile Crisis*. In calculating the correct course of action, weight must be given to the likely emotional reaction of the other party, particularly when the decision involves the potential destruction of humanity in a thermo-nuclear war, as was the case during the Cuban Missile Crisis.

You can also use the other parties' assumptions about your emotional state to your advantage if you are able to subsequently control your behaviour appropriately. A great example of this is when someone takes another person hostage and threatens to kill them if they do not reveal a key piece of information (such as buried treasure or safe codes). Like The Prisoner's Dilemma, this is a classic game theory set-up. The hostage knows that the captor will not kill them as they need the information and the captor knows that the hostage knows this so an impasse is reached. A logical solution for the captor is to signal a lack of emotional control which could potentially result in the captor executing the hostage out of anger or frustration. In this case, the hostage then fears that emotion could lead the captor to take a course of action not in their best interest. This may lead the hostage to give up the information if they are able to gain some surety that they will be unharmed once the information is given. Those who take others hostage are unlikely to be particularly trustworthy, so the hostage will have to construct a scenario which, depending on how important the information is, allows the hostage to escape with or without given the correct information. It is a bit off topic to go into this further here, however in simple terms this requires the introduction of two key scenarios – giving false information and/or creating a mechanism to provide safety once the information is verified correct.

Chapter Three – The Law of Karma

The law of karma, like the Four Noble Truths, is a central and key concept of Buddhist philosophy. The word 'karma' has been misused over the years; to the point where it's commonly accepted meaning in contemporary times has diverged from its true meaning. Karma has come to be known as some kind of *magical* universal force which rewards good and punishes evil. However this is not particularly accurate. The law of karma has many layers, including the concept of reincarnation, which is naturally beyond the scope of this discussion. Karma is basically the law of 'cause and effect', or, put in more specific terms, 'you reap what you sow'. Let me use the following example. Go and do something nice for someone like buy them a present or offer them a compliment. See how you feel afterwards. Now, by comparison, check how you feel next time you do something unpleasant or mean. You can even just imagine this and it has a similar physiological reaction. See how you feel after that. Unless you are a sociopath or suffering some other kind of personality disorder, you will clearly feel better when doing nice things. This is the law of karma at its most simple and basic.

Under the Eightfold Path of Buddhism, a key tenet is the concept of *Sila*, which means to act morally and to not harm others in any way. It can then be further broken down into the following guidelines, which I have tried to make as contemporary as possible -

1. Don't kill or harm living creatures
2. Don't steal
3. Don't get up to sexual hijinks which harm others
4. Don't tell lies or engage in mean spirited gossip
5. Don't get wasted on drugs and alcohol

The first thing you will notice is that for most of these guidelines, there will be grey areas. How do I kill animals to eat? Can I steal if I need food to survive? Can I have a one-night stand with someone if I am single? What should I say to my beefy wife if she asks me whether she looks fat in that dress? What about a single glass of red wine each night with dinner? I think the two key points to always look for are –

- Is this act harming anyone? (Either yourself or others)

- Is my motivation for committing this act wholesome or positive? There will always be anomalous exceptions which would provide good material for Buddhist scholars to debate, however in general these guidelines should be reasonably easy to follow.

I am not claiming anything particularly controversial or revolutionary by stating that if you follow these guidelines in both life and in business, you will be more successful over the long run. Contravening points 1, 2, 3 & 5 above are a sure-fire way to get yourself fired from your job or sent to jail for criminal or civil infractions. Point 4 will at the very least make you an unpopular person in your work or social environment.

In game theory, the concept of *credibility* is vital. This term has various applications in game theory. For example, a *non-credible threat* is a threatened action that no rational person would take. If I told you that if you didn't make me a sandwich I would cut off your arms and legs and roll you into a nearby river, this would be a *non-credible threat* as the threatened action is completely out of proportion with the context.

However, *credibility* can also refer to your reputation which has built up over time due to your many different actions and behaviours. The best example of this is the con-man. Once someone has gained the reputation as a con-man, apart from the fact that no-one wants to deal with them; they have also lost their ability to effectively outmanoeuvre their opponents in any interaction. Anything a con-man says cannot be considered true, making effective signalling for that person impossible.

This also brings up the important distinction between *repeated games* and *one-shot games*. A one-shot game is self-quarantined, with no future games dependent on its outcome. The previously mentioned Prisoner's Dilemma is a classic example of this. It makes no mention of each player's reputation which has built up over time. So, for example, if one of the players in the Prisoner's Dilemma was a known pathological liar and double-crosser, this would influence the choice of the other player.

However, in real life, repeated games tend to be the norm. The outcomes and behaviours identified in one particular game have influence over future, related games. Even interactions which seem, on face value, to be *one-shot*, are often not. To illustrate this I will return to my over-used example of buying a car. At first glance, if the salesman is able to trick the customer into paying too much or buying a lemon, it appears that this is *one-shot*, with no further implications. However, if this is repeated, gradually reputational risk increases as each cheated customer tells their friends or posts a complaint via a social network such as Facebook.

Where things get a little more complicated is in the area of *randomness*. In strategic interactions, you are typically advised to maintain a degree of randomness. This is most evident in sporting competitions which tend to be *zero-sum games* (there is a single winner and a single loser – plus one and minus one which net out at zero). If you are a baseball pitcher who always pitches a fastball, the batters will soon recognise this and will take advantage. Hence, there is a requirement to introduce randomness.

In business, randomness is also vital for success. If you always ask the seller to discount by $10, they will eventually just increase their price accordingly, knowing you will ask. I see this often in business dealings with Chinese companies. The Chinese have a strong haggling culture and like to finish on a price which has gone backwards and forwards several times in negotiation, before settling on a mid-point which is lower than the initial figure quoted. Western sellers often habituate to this and just start at a higher number than they would have otherwise done so. My recommendation to a Chinese company in this situation is to randomise. Sometimes haggle, sometimes book the business at a higher number (with a tendency to do these on smaller deals) and importantly, sometimes just walk away from the negotiation after receiving the first price from the seller.

Where this gets complicated is the fine line between *randomising* and outright lying. I think the guiding principle should be – *Am I causing harm by these actions?* Even this question leads you to a grey area. If you successfully negotiate with someone so that you get an additional monetary or non-monetary benefit, is this harming them? For this I think you need to accept the flow of money back and forth due to negotiation as being a given in commercial life. The key is whether your actions lead to additional negative consequences like someone getting fired or a company going bankrupt. I like to use the somewhat odd analogy of a virus. Interacting in a repeated commercial arrangement with another party, you need to fashion yourself on a benign Influenza virus strain that doesn't kill the host, instead of the Spanish Flu or Ebola, which kills the host. This doesn't help anyone.

By following the guidelines of *Sila*, you will be maximising your success in repeated games. Others will not be on high-alert when interacting with you and you will be able to effectively signal, knowing that your words and actions are credible. A person's professional life is a perfect microcosm to witness the law of karma in effect. Whilst there is a stereotypical image of the ambitious and Machiavellian executive who has back-stabbed his way to the top, in reality this is an exceedingly rare scenario. The person who cultivates close relationships, treats people with respect and acts with a strong moral compass is more likely to succeed in a business environment. Seeing *Person A* treat *Person B* badly, only to see *Person B* end up as the boss of *Person A* and make their life hell, is one of the more exquisite examples of the law of Karma in action.

The law of Karma also has an entirely different aspect which is unrelated to the question of behaviour and morality, and this is where the parallels with game theory are strongest. game theory and Karma are focused on the same thing – gaining a clear understanding of the effects of various decisions and actions.

One thing I noticed from my own various Buddhist practices was that I have slowly gained a better ability to map out a chain of cause and effect from a particular point in time. This is particularly so regarding conflict and acts which arise out of anger. Some of my biggest regrets from a professional perspective have been when I have acted (either subtly or overtly) out of anger. Of all the emotions, anger would have to be the most acutely destructive. A single angry word or action can set in motion a chain of events with startlingly dramatic consequences. However, this can be short circuited by a clear understanding of the law of Karma.

Where this intersects with game theory is when you need to map out the various ways in which a particular scenario can play out. game theory provides the framework to empirically capture the effects of each decision and its impact on the other player or counter-party. A decision tree is used to represent each decision and its effects in an extensive-form game, that is, a scenario involving several different moves by each party.

I will deliberately avoid going into the various permutations of the decision tree as it is not my intention to recreate what has already been explained elsewhere by those more knowledgeable than myself in this area. However what I will say is that if you need to map out a scenario with multiple options and multiple steps, the decision tree is the best way known to capture this. The key point is that you need to get into the habit of looking into the chain of cause and effect past the initial move. Often, it will then be clear as to which course of action is the most appropriate in that particular situation. Depending on the scenario, you can also use squares or circles at each *node* to represent whether it is a *decision node* (mapping your choice) or a *chance node* (mapping the opponent's potential moves).

The beauty of Buddhist practice in this area is the extent to which it can help you develop the skill to see a scenario with clarity. Buddhist study of cause and effect is incredibly nuanced, especially regarding the theme of *Pratityasamutpada*, which is roughly translated as dependent origination. The concept of dependent origination says that even the term *cause and effect* is misleading as it suggests a single cause leading to a single effect. Reality is considerably more complex. At one level, dependent origination can be thought of as another way to represent chaos theory, or the butterfly effect. As you would probably know, the butterfly effect (apart from being an Ashton Kutcher thriller of dubious merit from 2004) says that a butterfly can flap its wings in one part of the world which eventually causes a hurricane in another part. Everything is interrelated and nothing *originates* independently.

The concept of dependent origination also has links through to physics and the concepts of 'determinism' and 'free will'. In his famous piece (well, at least in physics and philosophy circles – it's no *Fifty Shades of Grey*) *A Philosophical Essay on Probabilities*, French mathematician Pierre Simon Laplace stated – *"We may regard the present state of the universe as the effect of its past and the cause of its future".*

Laplace posited a theoretical being, which subsequently came to be known as *Laplace's Demon*, who was completely omniscient, knowing absolutely everything in the universe down to the smallest detail. Laplace proposed that, if such a being existed at the time of the Big Bang, it could predict the entire future of the universe down to the smallest details. For example, if such a being existed, it would have known at the time of the Big Bang that you would be here reading a mediocre book on Zen and game theory at this moment in time. Or to put it in Buddhist perspective, the concept of dependent origination would mean that this being could map out the chain of cause and effect from the Big Bang onwards until the end of time.

Now, on reading about *Laplace's Demon*, after thinking for a few minutes you may be struck with the same thought which has outraged opponents of determinism since the concept was raised many years ago – if this being knew everything at the point of the big bang, where does that leave free will? I thought free will drove me to make a cup of coffee just then? If not, who actually decided to make a cup of coffee? Me? Fortunately (if you believe in free will), in recent years, quantum mechanics has come to the rescue with concepts such as the *Heisenberg Uncertainty Principle* and *Schrödinger's Cat*. I won't got into too much detail, lest your eyes glaze over, however at the very least, Schrödinger's Cat is something worth mentioning. Both the *Uncertainty Principle* and *Schrödinger's Cat* both concern themselves with the belief that at the quantum or subatomic level, events become impossible to predict with the level of confidence we have for larger objects.

To illustrate this concept, Erwin Schrödinger proposed a thought experiment where a cat is sealed in an opaque box along with a deadly apparatus. The apparatus is set up in a way so that if a single atom of a radioactive substance in the box decays, the apparatus will kill the cat with cyanide. Remember that the box is sealed with no way of knowing what is transpiring or has transpired inside. The key point is that the decay of radioactive atoms is unpredictable with any degree of certainty according to any methods of measurement we have. Here is where

Schrödinger's Cat gets interesting. According to the thought experiment, until you open the box, the cat is both dead and alive at the same time at the quantum level! This is due to the fact that the decay of the radioactive material in the box cannot be predicted with any accuracy.

So, accordingly, many opponents of determinism use the example of quantum dynamics to refute the complete absence of free will. Currently, thought experiments such as these are viewed as paradoxes. However things will get very interesting if, one day, our tools of measurement or technology advances to the point where we can remove the 'uncertainty' from quantum dynamics. Then we are back at *Laplace's Demon* again!

So, from the Buddhist perspective, the key takeaway from this is that everything is interrelated. Nothing happens in a vacuum. To use Laplace's original idea, whatever you see in front of you is the result of an immeasurable (unless you are said Demon) chain of cause and effect. Another way to express this concept is via the food on your table in front of you. Look at your dinner and think about all the different causes and effects which transpired to create it. Just take the steak for example. A cow had to be slaughtered by someone, that cow had to be fed, someone had to grow the grain used to feed the cow, someone had to produce the fertilizer for those crops, someone had to invest in the fertilizer plant and so on – and that is just for the steak! That steak you are looking at is the *effect* of countless *causes* leading all the way back to the Big Bang (and beyond). Try to think of something in the universe which is not the effect of multiple previous actions or events. You cannot – everything is interrelated.

Now, for the purposes of formulating various strategies and mapping out their consequences, your obviously do not need to trace everything back as far as the Big Bang. However, it is important to practice looking at a scenario deeply to capture all the various events which have led to your current scenario and all the different consequences, not just the overt primary *effect* which results from each choice.

From a strategic perspective, the most common error I see people make in business is that they believe their strategy occurs in a vacuum – *"Our competitor is doing X so we should beat them by doing Y"*. That's all well and good but what happens when you start doing Y? What will be your competitor's reaction? They are not going to just declare *"OK, you beat us, we surrender"*. They are going to then do something in response to your X. You need to map this out when deciding a course of action. Failure to do this is usually the cause of pointless strategies such as price wars – *"Our competitor charges $10, so we will take their market share by charging $9"*. This is all well and good if you know your competitor's cost of production is $9.50, but what if you are taking on the market leader who is at the cheapest end of the cost curve? They can just drop their price to $8 and put you out of business. Properly mapping this out beforehand would avoid costly mistakes such as these.

Chapter Four - Impermanence

It is a great testament to the startlingly original concepts first proposed by the Buddha, over two thousand years ago, that many have only recently been validated by modern science. One of the best examples of this is the concept of anitya, or impermanence, which is central to Buddhist thought and philosophy. Anitya states that all conditioned phenomena are subject to decay and dissolution. By *conditioned*, it means any compound state. Remember, this concept pre-dates the term entropy and the second law of thermodynamics by over two thousand years!

A good example of this is the human body, an extremely complex *compound* object. The natural process of aging is the perfect representation of the theory of impermanence. The human body is in a constant state of flux. In fact, as your various cells & organs replace themselves, the body you have today contains very little of the body you had a year ago. A lot of biological effort goes into holding what is a highly complex compound organism together, so over time the natural forces of entropy will eventually win. Your telomeres shorten, your immune system makes mistakes and the natural process of apoptosis (programmed cell death) occasionally stays switched on – leading to cancer.

The Buddha identified that the human mind tends to ascribe permanence to impermanent objects, most commonly regarding the human life. We are born, we grow old and we die in the blink of an eye in the overall scheme of things. However on a day to day basis there is a sub-conscious belief that we are permanent. This can be by the denial of our own death or by the belief in an eternal, unchanging *soul*. As a side note, for those of you depressed or disheartened by all this talk regarding the lack of a soul, the concept of *soul* leaves a lot of room for interpretation. Buddhism does state that *something* is reincarnated after death, however the definition of what that 'something' might be, is where the debate lies. Even within differing sects of Buddhism this point is (some may say pointlessly) debated.

It is this lack of clarity of thought regarding impermanence which then permeates the area of commercial strategy. What do the following companies have in common – Kodak, Blockbuster, General Motors, Lehman Brothers, Merrill Lynch and Bear Stearns? Each of these companies has at one time or another dominated their industry and seemed indestructible. However each one of them has either collapsed, encountered a near-death experience or currently operates as a shadow of its former glory. There are also companies today who are showing signs of vulnerability after previously appearing unassailable. For more than 20 years, Microsoft has dominated the world of personal computers via its *Windows* desktop operating system. Despite the best intentions of challengers such as Linux, Microsoft's hegemony in this space seemed fixed in stone. However with the advent of the tablet computer, namely Apple's *iPad*, Windows suddenly appears fallible as the default operating system used by consumers worldwide. That's not to say that Microsoft is on the downward spiral to inevitable oblivion; however what was previously inconceivable is now less so.

Nowhere is the concept of impermanence more applicable than the cellular phone & smart phone market, where the usual processes of obsolescence and the dominance of certain companies appears to be accelerated. Fifteen years ago, everybody I knew used a Nokia cell phone. Fast forward to 2013 and Nokia is doubtful as a going concern, its stock dropping almost 95% since 2007. In business, Nokia phones were replaced with BlackBerrys, making the Canadian manufacturer Research in Motion (RIM) the fastest growing company in the world in 2009. BlackBerrys were so ubiquitous that they earned the nickname "Crackberry" as their owners became so attached to them that they could not stop checking emails on them. However, just 3 years later, due to the emergence of the Apple iPhone and the Samsung Galaxy range, RIM is now itself in danger of bankruptcy.

As you may have noticed by looking at the different examples I have given for companies which have fallen by the wayside, there are two general ways which impermenence exerts its inescapable power in the corporate arena – failure due to competitive pressures and *Black Swan* events. The above examples of Nokia, Kodak and RIM are classic examples of a company not innovating. They are victims of impermanence in its classic form – the world changed around them and they failed to adapt.

Black Swan refers to events which are unpredictable but which can have disproportionately large consequences. The term was popularized by famed epistemologist Nassim Nicholas Taleb to describe certain events which occur despite huge statistical improbability. Taleb gained fame in the wake of the Global Financial Crisis (GFC) as he correctly warned about the fragility of the financial system at the time, particularly the huge mortgage companies Fannie Mae and Freddy Mac. These warnings eventually proved prescient. One of the key themes of Taleb's book is that human beings consistently underestimate the likelihood of Black Swan events occurring. It is this undeniable truth which has proved the folly of many people whose job it is to mathematically model risk. Whether it is the GFC or the collapse of companies such as Long Term Credit Management and Enron, if someone modelled the risk of the event actually occurring, the probabilities would have seemed astronomical.

For the purposes of this discussion, they key message is that with a large enough quantum of time and a large enough sample size, seemingly improbable events with large consequences ARE going to happen. Remember that dinosaurs ruled the earth for around 135 million years before they were wiped out by massive, fiery Black Swan in the shape of an asteroid which struck the earth around 66 million years ago. To put this in perspective, Homo sapiens emerged only 200,000 years ago, so we must survive all the various Black Swan events that may come our way for another 134 million years just to match the dinosaurs' reign. Considering that we now possess the ability to completely destroy ourselves via nuclear, chemical or biological weaponry, it makes the likelihood of this appear remote. Without wanting to appear too negative, all it may take during those 134 million years would be a single psychopath with access to weapons of mass destruction to wipe the human race off the face of the planet. Add to this the spectre of asteroids and climate change, our chances of long term survival appear remote. Plus, remember that these are just the events that we can conceive of. Our "known unknowns" as Donald Rumsfeld would call them. It is quite possible that we will be wiped out by something which is currently inconceivable (our "unknown unknowns", such as the planet suddenly being taken over by Antarctic marine krill or the human race spontaneously developing an allergic reaction to carbon.

The failure of many strategies and companies themselves can be traced back to this failure in grasping this inherent instability of phenomena. The situation is in a constant state of flux both at a micro level (such as a negotiation or series of negotiations with a customer or partner) and a macro level (the overall viability of a company due to a change in the operating environment).

Indeed, companies and the people that they are constructed of, have an under-recognised tendency to be strategically inflexible. This is particularly so regarding the establishment of a business plan or strategy at an arbitrary point in the year which is then following with unwavering commitment, irrespective of any changes to the environment. Almost two hundred years ago, German Field Marshall Helmuth von Moltke famously stated *"No battle plan survives first contact with the enemy"*. If your entire plan is based on the enemy initially flanking right and they flank left, what ongoing utility does your plan provide?

Things change - consumer preferences, economic conditions, supply and demand are all in a state of flux. All these things are not static and require both astute observation and a framework for strategic flexibility. By way of example, an Equities Analyst (someone who analyses different companies with a view to providing stock picks) is someone who must embody all the requirements mentioned here. They must keep abreast of all developments (changes) which may require a change to existing investment advice and they must map out the chain of cause and effect. A prospective stock picker who wishes to invest successfully for their own personal wealth must also follow these principles. The best of example of this at work is the effects which large macro events affect individual stock prices. Whilst it seemed macabre and insensitive, in the wake of the Fukushima nuclear disaster, the price of uranium miners' stocks dropped and LNG producers rose as the market predicted a switch from nuclear to natural gas as a result of that incident. There are constantly occurring both Black Swan events and gradual changes which require dexterity at both the personal and corporate level. A failure to recognise this inherent impermanence can be disastrous.

Chapter Five – The Middle Way

Before the Buddha's famed enlightenment under the Bodhi tree, a little over 2000 years ago, he spent a period engaging in ascetic practices which were common at that time in India. It was thought at that time that spiritual awakening would come via extreme practices such as extended fasting and self-mortification. By following these practices, such as by reputedly consuming only a single leaf each day, the Buddha's health gradually deteriorated before, near-death, he experienced a key realisation one day – the key to enlightenment comes via *The Middle Way*, avoiding extremes of self-mortification and self-indulgence.

These days, this is no longer such a revolutionary concept, with a focus on balance being strongly promoted in the many aspects of commercial life. Whilst there are some select exceptions, in general, the application of *balance* will be the default best option for the majority of endeavours.

One of the best applications for this concept is regarding work ethic. Despite the proliferation of expressions such as *work smarter, not harder*, giving any endeavour less than 100% at all times remains a pejorative concept. This is irrespective of the actual benefit gained. This concept is discussed at length by author Richard Koch in his book, *Living the 80/20 Way*. Koch has popularised what is known as *Pareto's Principle* which says (in this context), 80% of your rewards will come from 20% of your efforts. The remaining 20% of your efforts are wasted. (As an aside, this reminds me of an oft-used quote in marketing from a fabled CEO – "*I know 50% of my advertising is wasted, but I don't know which 50%!*" – You may say a similar thing when *Pareto's Principle* tells you that 80% of your efforts are wasted. Identifying which 80% is part of the challenge!). If the law of diminishing returns says that, in a given activity, past a certain sweet-spot, working an extra 80% harder will give you an extra 2% return, should you go for it or throttle your effort back to the sweet spot? Well, this depends on the endeavour. For one-shot, high importance events, it makes sense to give the full 100%. It makes little sense to throttle effort if you are in the final at Wimbledon. However if you are, say, Roger Federer and about to play in your round 1 match, it would make little sense to give 100% and leave nothing on the court. The correct medium term strategy for Roger is to carefully apply the right level of effort depending on the occasion. Assuming all other factors being equal, this will allow him to reach the final in the best possible condition to win. Tennis is a fantastic arena to apply game theory principles and this is no exception. We can introduce a further complication to the above plan – what if Roger throttles effort in order to preserve his physical condition and as a result he gets drawn into five-set matches? It is here that you see how important it is to correctly apply the right amount of effort. In many sporting endeavours it is a key focus of training to be able to apply the right amount of effort by neither going too hard too early or by slackening off too much and putting victory out of grasp. This is a recurring theme in endurance events such as marathons and cycling. To be fair, recently in cycling they have applied the Middle Way differently – taking just enough steroids that they help you to win but not so much so they are detectable.

Despite the *work smarter, not harder* mantra, it remains frowned upon if you are viewed as not giving '100%' all the time. Scottish historian Niall Ferguson traces this back to the *Protestant work ethic*, which emphasised hard work and frugality as a means to please God and enter heaven. Ferguson has even linked the domination of the West over the East back to this key trait.

Fortunately the expression 'work/life balance' is becoming widespread as companies realise that by enforcing a kind of Middle Way with their employees' habits, they avoid burnout and keep productivity high. Remember, 'work/life balance' is not HR-speak for *slacking off*. In fact, *slacking off* is a perfect expression for applying Middle Way principles. A great analogy is that of a guitar string. With the tension too tight there is a risk of the string snapping and with the tension too loose the string cannot produce anything. Similarly, a work environment with not enough to do and no stressful or challenging situations is also a recipe for disaster. The key is balance. The target should be a stimulating environment, achievable & measurable goals, acute controlled stress and adequate downtime. Acute and controlled stress is good for you. It activates the motivation and reward centres in the brain. The key points are duration and control. If your job is permanently and unrelentingly stressful, you will be on a fast track to a nervous breakdown. However, if you have intermittent periods of stress (such as pitching for a new client or trying to land a big deal) with commensurate periods of rest, you will be practicing Middle Way principles to perfection. The other key aspect is control. A lack of control puts an animal or person at risk of developing anxiety disorders or depression. Multiple tests have shown that when you take away an animal's sense of control, anxiety and depression follows. The classic experiment is where a mouse is set up in an environment where there is a source of electric shocks. If the mouse can take some form of action to control the shocks, they maintain relative control. If the mouse is subjected to random shocks over which it exerts no control, biomarkers of anxiety and depression result.

This has also been replicated in studies on groups of animals. Dominant male primates show higher levels of serotonin than the submissive males, which is believe to result from the lack of control over their own destiny such as through the choice of mate or access to the best food. These studies have been extrapolated to comparisons with humans in a company environment. People with control over their environment, particularly those in positions of power due to success, demonstrate generally better mental health than those who remain stuck in *dead-end* roles at the bottom of the company hierarchy.

In my own personal experience, the *work smarter, not harder* philosophy has appeared to be, in general, the better option for long term success. The most successful people I know have not necessarily been the smartest or the hardest working. They have a gift for applying just the right amount of effort at just the right time, over the course of their life. Be strategic in how to approach any endeavour. Is it a sprint? Is it a marathon? Is it important in the long run?

If you find yourself experiencing automatic guilty thoughts due to the throttling of effort, you need to rationalise it as follows – I am not being lazy, I am stockpiling effort and energy to apply to a more appropriate endeavour.

The other key point is that high-quality, inspiring work emerges from joy. Toil and drudgery are rarely the wellspring of creativity. The famous Vietnamese Zen priest Thich Nhat Hanh, who is always a source of great succinct quotes, says *"If your practice does not bring you joy, you are not practicing correctly"*. This is directed at spiritual practise and meditation in particular. He is saying you should follow the Middle Way, avoiding hard, ascetic practices, yet still applying enough effort to keep your passion alive. This can be applied to any endeavour. Too little effort and you will be bored, too much and you will be overwhelmed. Follow the Middle Way and you will ensure the right conditions for genuine inspiration and success to emerge.

Chapter Six – Non-Harm

Early game theory was heavily skewed towards a very singular theme – how to utilise probability and strategic thought to maximise personal gain. However, increasingly, there has been a great deal of focus on the concept of co-operating to maximise gain for both. Or put another way – the other side doesn't have to fail for you to win.

As mentioned earlier, many people are stuck in the overly binary "zero-sum game" mind-set, where there is a winner and a loser, with no shades of grey or synergies to be achieved. It is clear that when we look closely, much of commercial and personal life is enhanced when each party co-operates with the other. Now, this doesn't mean that in all cases there is scope for co-operation. There will still be cases where co-operation does not make either short term or long term sense for one or both of the parties. Furthermore, there are also cases where co-operation is disallowed – such as with anti-trust legislation that prohibits anti-competitive collusion.

Let me give an example of beneficial co-operation that would be extremely common. Say you have a seller and a buyer, who engage in commercial transactions on a repeat basis. From both a strategic and ethical perspective, there is one general course of action that makes sense for both – *Concede when the other side has more to lose than you have to gain or more to gain than you have to lose.*

Principles of Influence

Noted psychology and marketing expert Robert Cialdini, details a range of what he calls "principles of influence" which underpin his overall philosophy of exerting influence – primarily for commercial gain. Two of these principles illustrate perfectly the consequences of co-operating ethically with your competitor.

Firstly, he mentions "reciprocity", which basically means that when you do something nice or benevolent for someone, that party naturally feels the need to return the favour. Social psychologists have known this for a long time and often cite Hare Krishna followers as the perfect example. When Hare Krishna members are trying to get the message out, they will invariably do something that is not necessarily purely out the kindness of their heart. They will first give you something, perhaps pointing out that it is free, so no payment required. They do this because they know that many people are bound by the principle of reciprocity. Either consciously or unconsciously, there will be a mental process along the lines of *"Well he did give me this beautiful flower, so I guess I owe it to him to hear him out."*

If you concede a minor point to your competition, they will usually feel bound by the same principle, to a degree.

Put another way, if you screw the other guy, he is going to screw you back. In game theory this is referred to as "tit for tat", and is a powerful motivator. Tit for tat is the equal and opposite of reciprocity. Namely, do something nice for the other party and they will feel often feel compelled to return the favour. Do something uncooperative or refuse to concede a minor point, tit for tat can be the likely outcome. Whether you have pure, ethical motivations or are just motivated by an aversive fear of tit for tat, cooperation in commercial life is almost always the best long term strategy.

To put this visually, imagine two overlapping circles, each representing two parties in a commercial relationship. The overlapping area is where the interests of each party converge and they should be co-operating. When you take a long term view, this area of overlap is much larger than most people assume.

The other principle that Cialdini mentions is "Liking", which essentially refers to the fact that people are inclined to do nice things for people they like. Again this has been backed up by multiple behavioural studies which have consistently shown the same principle – even when it is not in their logical best interest, people will often feel more inclined to do something nice for someone they like.

I have seen this principle at work on an extremely common basis. At each company I have worked at, there are always unpleasant counterparties that my company has to deal with. Either they are unpleasant people to deal with or their company has a particular philosophy which doesn't recognise either "reciprocity" or "liking". What invariably occurs is that the commercial staff in my company will imbue commercial transactions with a degree of spite. One work colleague of mine always charged what he called an "asshole tax" to a particularly difficult customer he dealt with. The problem is that this just leads to tit for tat. On the other side of this coin, another customer was a prototypical "sweet old lady" who was a joy to work with. This same colleague would often make large concessions or sell too cheaply to this same lady, simply because he liked her so much.

What about psychopaths?

One thing you may be thinking while reading this is – *What about all those sociopaths that end up as the CEO of the company?*

This is a little more complicated that first glance would suggest. Remember, psychopathy is a rare aberration for a good reason. If we return to the original example of a caveman cooperating with another caveman to bring down a large animal, we can clearly see how psychopathy has clear limitations. Yes, perhaps the psychopath may realise that he needs to cooperate with the other caveman to get a meal. But longer term, psychopaths invariably leave a trail of destruction behind them. Yes, a small minority are able to control or hide their destructive urges enough to become a CEO, but a larger proportion end up either societal rejects or in prison.

Many situations require a degree of co-operation which psychopaths find difficult. Furthermore, many of these situations are set up so that acts of malice or lack of co-operation will be followed by retribution which is grossly out of proportion with the original act. Put another way, if you act like an asshole, people will be even bigger assholes back to you. Again this has been borne out by multiple studies. If someone inflicts damage on another person (whether commercial, physical or social) equal to "1", that person will invariably try to inflict "1+x" back to the original person.

This has solid grounding in evolutionary psychology as, throughout history, humans needed other humans to act in a cooperative and harmonious fashion. This is particularly the case where a particular endeavour benefits the whole tribe or village and individuals can benefit even if they do not contribute. For example, if the village builds a fence around the perimeter to keep wild animals out and certain individuals refuse to assist, despite the fact that they will benefit equally. We are strongly wired to react to this scenario with either retribution or by socially ostracising the offender.

As I mentioned previously, as long as the net result is cooperation, kindness and a lack of suffering, I believe the motivations are less important. Of course, as a long-term endeavour, the goal of acting out of pure "*lovingkindness*" (in the Buddhist sense) is a worthy one. Perhaps over many years of practicing *Tonglen* (or similar "*lovingkindness* meditations") you can eventually get to this hallowed mind-space. However, for the meantime, as long as your actions embody the spirit of cooperation and don't harm others, I think this is a pretty darn good start.

Conclusion

This book does not contain any magic information that will guarantee you become a CEO or a billionaire. What it does contain is some general concepts that can be applied to different aspects of your life. If I could distil the content down to some key points it would be -

- Gain control over your emotions to ensure you act logically and in your best interest
- Gain control over your levels of attachment to various events and scenarios
- Learn to map out the chain of cause and effect of various decisions and events
- When you gain true understanding of the law of cause and effect, you will realise that you should always act morally, ethically and without causing harm to others
- Things change, so you need to adapt accordingly
- Practice *balance* in all aspects of life
- Learn to cooperate with others, for your mutual long term benefit

It is no use being on your deathbed knowing that you outsmarted everyone, leaving a trail of misery and destruction like the psychopaths I mentioned previously. Anyone can grab a gun and rob their opponent of $100. However, if, via your application of clever strategic principles and ethical action, you can engineer it so that both you and your opponent have $100 each, that is the real challenge and a true marker of greatness.

Recommended Reading

Game theory

Thinking Strategically: The Competitive Edge in Business, Politics, and Everyday Life by Avinash K. Dixit and Barry J. Nalebuff (Apr 17, 1993)

The Art of Strategy: A game Theorist's Guide to Success in Business and Life by Avinash K. Dixit and Barry J. Nalebuff (Jan 4, 2010)

Game theory for Business: A Primer in Strategic Gaming by Paul Papayoanou (Dec 10, 2010)

Buddhism & Mindfulness

Mindfulness for Beginners: Reclaiming the Present Moment - and Your Life by Jon Kabat-Zinn (Dec 28, 2011)

Peace Is Every Step: The Path of Mindfulness in Everyday Life by Thich Nhat Hanh, Arnold Kotler and H. H. the Dalai Lama (Mar 1, 1992)

Zen Mind, Beginner's Mind by Shunryu Suzuki and David Chadwick (Jun 28, 2011)

General

The Black Swan: The Impact of the Highly Improbable by Nassim Nicholas Taleb (Apr 3, 2008)

Fooled by Randomness: The Hidden Role of Chance in Life and in the Markets by Nassim Nicholas Taleb (Oct 14, 2008)

The Misbehavior of Markets: A Fractal View of Financial Turbulence by Benoit Mandelbrot and Richard L. Hudson (Mar 7, 2006)

The Logic of Scientific Discovery (Routledge Classics) by Karl Raimund Popper (Mar 29, 2002)

Thinking, Fast and Slow by Daniel Kahneman (Oct 25, 2011)

When Genius Failed: The Rise and Fall of Long-Term Capital Management by Roger Lowenstein (Oct 9, 2001)

www.ingramcontent.com/pod-product-compliance
Lightning Source LLC
Chambersburg PA
CBHW071525180526
45171CB00002B/387